fire, salt, light

Melissa Anderson

For

Jeff, Lauren & Julia
My whole world
Thank you for showing me
what love is and how
it can transform
e v e r y t h i n g

CONTENTS

ACKNOWLEDGEMENTS

First and foremost, thank you to Sierra Harris and Karen Richard, without whom this book would not exist. Thank you to Sierra for seeing something in my story and my words that prompted you to want to bring them to life in this way. I am honoured and grateful. Thank you to Karen for tirelessly working on the technical and creative details, while being incredibly thoughtful and mindful of my vision throughout the process. It has been a privilege to work with you and witness your gifts in action. Thank you to both Sierra and Karen for seeing my vision from day one and the heart with which I wanted this project to be received. I can't thank you enough.

Thank you to my brother, Joel, and his wonderful wife, Anjuli, for facilitating the relationship that led to the creation of this book and for always supporting me in my writing journey and in all I do. Thank you to my sister, Wendy, for loving and supporting me always. It is a blessing to have a brother and sister I can call two of my closest friends. Thank you to Wendy and Jess for being my sounding boards throughout this process. Thank you for providing creative input and helping me remain true to my vision throughout this process. Jess, you are family and my sister in every true sense of the word; thank you for being one of my greatest cheerleaders from day one. Thank you to my loving parents for being so supportive of me and my love of writing since I was a young girl, and always making sure I have no end to journals, even still today. To my in-laws for supporting and loving me like their own daughter. Thank you to my sister-in-law, Heidi, for always encouraging me to write and for sharing your knowledge as a songwriter. Thank you to Anna, for blessing me with the type of friendship that changes me and encourages me to be a better person, and to Alyssa for being an encourager and a constant in my life. Thank you to all my friends and family for seeing in me what I sometimes couldn't see in myself. I love all of you.

Thank you to the Instagram poetry community for the unending support you have given me these last few years. Thank you for being a safe space for me to share, create, and experiment. I will forever treasure the friendships and connections I've made. Thank you to every literary magazine, journal and website that has published my works. It has given me the courage to keep sharing. Thank you to Rupi Kaur for the beautiful writing exercise of "Dear Younger Me," which resulted in one of the pieces I share in the book. Thank you to the many authors and poets I look up to and admire, including Mary Oliver and Morgan Harper Nichols, two of the many whose works bring light to this world and make the kind of difference I could only hope to one day.

Thank you to my husband, Jeff, and our daughters, Lauren and Julia, without whom none of this would be possible. Thank you for loving me, for encouraging me, and for reminding me what is most important in life. My girls, you inspire me more than you will ever know. You are everything this world needs and I love you more than words could say. Jeff, because of you I know a great love most will never know. There is no shortage of things to write about because of the beautiful life we've built together. I love you.

I am grateful for the Grace that has brought me here, and for the peace and joy I experience in any circumstance, even the most difficult ones.

Finally, thank you, Dear Reader. Thank you for holding my book and for reading my words. I hope they make a home somewhere in your heart. Even if just for a while.

Love,
Melissa

firstlight

There are so many little joys each day.

So many moments where time all but stops.

Like an aperture setting,

I focus in and everything else fades away.

I hold there, slowing my breath, pausing.

Storing this moment away somewhere

deep inside, knowing

I'll need to call it back one particularly dark day

when light has gone.

On a day I forget

I control aperture.

the early september sun reaches out to me this autumn morning, stretching across the room to this old well-loved table. *feel me* it seems to beg. *see me.* remember me in this moment and the warmth i freely give. now go. be a light today. *feel, see, remember, give.* and tomorrow, r i s e and do the same.

become l o v e

and watch   the

world   around

you   bend

toward light

i'm learning to lighten my grip on most

everything. believing what is meant for me will

always remain. and what is not will gently fall

a w a y.

i hope you always find me

in the little moments

most people miss

may i learn to seek
more of what i need
and less of what i want

may i forever seek to be *kinder,*
to be more *present,* to be
someone who leaves the world
and people b e t t e r than i
found them.

i tend not

to pay attention

to whether the glass

is half-full or half-empty

i'm simply grateful for the water

art doesn't cover pain. it greets it. it asks

for nothing. not to be understood, or even

loved. only seen. it brings me into the fold

of all that i am and everything i long to be.

it reminds me to be a noticer of unnoticed

things.

even here

i will seek joy

—even here

your existence is a miracle.

walk gently with its gift.

c e r t a i n t y

is but an

i l l u s i o n

and so

it is

f a i t h

i choose each day

our mutual freedom
requires us to brave
our darkness and
stoke our light

you feel like sunday

and sundays are

e v e r y t h i n g

to me

once you learn you
deserve more, you
accept nothing less

there is no part of you

undeserving of the

s u n

moonrise

i feel it again. the warmth of autumn
burning its final flame. each day i hold
on to it - *gently*. savouring it. but i feel it.
winter's edge reaching beyond autumn's,
settling in quietly. darkness creeping in
earlier each evening, staying later each
morning. *i let it*. i don't fear it. and i
don't become it. for i have always known
we are far more light than dark.

Winter made its last stand yesterday, and this morning, the sun is once again bright and well-placed. I feel the longing in the blue sky that holds her. The promise of spring is in her rise, and I allow hope to rise with her. I sow seeds of patience and walk each row. Spring is fluent in purpose. Fulfilling hers each day. Inspiring me to fulfill mine.

i want to feel the sun again
to sleep under a loving moon
i want to feel the earth carry me
and the sky blanket me

but for now

i will let this sadness hold me
just a while

you are my moon
i am your tide
you keep pulling me
to you

in the rise and fall of all that is

let me be your moon, your sun

i surrender my soul

to   september

carrying   all   of

august's   warmth

tucked beneath my

skin

i long for this ache to be replaced

for lightness and freedom to take its place

but

just as you cannot rush the tide

nor the seasons

you cannot rush healing

so

i will let each feeling come

i will feel all that needs to be felt

then i will let it s

             e

               t with the sun

                    on this prairie horizon

v a s t and e n d l e s s

is this love

the way the moon belongs to the

night

the sun to the sky

so you belong

y o u   b e l o n g

how quickly we are to forget

we are all branches of the

same tree

let's paint castles in the sky

with fingertips

let's forever stay

just like this

let memories f a d e

until all we see

is here and now

until all we are

is *love*

body still and quiet
mind a raging sea
these sleepless nights
steal the light away from me
physically i'm resting
mentally i'm wrestling
wishing for morning
while secretly dreading her
and her sun

it took me quite some time to learn

that this tender heart

and sensitive soul

are gifts wrapped in cloud paper

delicate and transparent

but worth the pain

just to watch the way

the sun shines through

i've been drawing maps
and charting stars
and all roads lead to you

where once she read poetry

soaked up its warmth

bathed in its waters

now it invades

her every dream

it speaks to her in low hums

and wild reckonings

heartlines

there is much to be said on falling in love,

and little on *living* in love,

                  resting in love,

                          being in love.

the falling seems more poetic,

                          intoxicating.

but those who have lived in love may know,

the true poetry is found in the *living*.

                        in the *being*.

in knowing the falling is temporary,

but the staying, and the choosing

        {{ l o v e }}

is always.

and maybe,

that is all the poetry we will ever need.

when i said, 'i do'
i had no idea how much
i'd love you one day
i thought that was the peak of it
but i was so wrong

i loved you, yes
but now
i love every part of you
i didn't know then
i love the you who wasn't yet

I know not what it takes to heal a
world
but I have a feeling it begins with
L O V E

in the folds of this heartache

lies the strength to pull me through

for there is no heartache that

did not first begin as love

and there is no love that

did not first begin as you

i do not take for granted the love

you so freely give, nor how safe i

feel to be completely and *exactly*

who i a m.

you brought me sunshine

on my darkest days

a bouquet of love

a gift of grace

and so i thank you

for all the ways

you love me

i think it's a

brave, brave thing

the way you love

like your heart has never been

broken

what if heart strings

were made to be pulled

beautifully unravelled

gently collected

perfectly pooled

at the feet of those

who need love most

i wonder
if i were to stretch
one arm east
and one arm west
would the world feel
my warm embrace

find me in the hidden places
i am the love letters tucked inside your novels
i am the dried flowers between your pages

when you feel hollow
a shell of who you once were
remember all the room
it leaves for love

i hope

when   you   read   my

words

you *feel* me

just a little

m o r e

i hope my heart

makes   a   home   in

yours

for just a while

for just a while

and they say

but the world is too cold

love won't be enough

to make it warm

and i say

no

but maybe it will be

enough to light a spark

and maybe that spark will be

enough to cause more of us to start a fire

— start fires

don't get so caught up

loving someone

that you forget

you are someone, too

to be seen as we are

and not as we could be

that is the love we all seek

finding hope in the moments when i've lost my breath

finding stillness in the chaos and commotion

finding grace in the currents of judgement

in a world screaming that it's not enough

— *wholly loved, forever seen*

The longing for more,
for something more
beautiful   tucked
beneath our skin.

healingtides

beautifully broken

to let the light in

don't let your scars

keep you from your calling

scars run deep

courage runs deeper

i knew

               you were different

the moment

        you turned

                { { toward } }

my *pain*

                        and not   a w a y

those who have faced life-shattering pain
their hearts broken open wide
can't help but see your pain
they see it in the slight rounding of your shoulders
in the way you run your fingers along seams
— over and over
they know the subtle pause before you answer when
you're asked if you're okay
their own pain has made them unable to look away

i try to untangle grief from love

but the two cannot be separated

when grief only exists *because* of

l o v e

i can love you

but i can't heal you

i can hold you

but i can't make you whole

and perhaps that is

the most difficult part of it all

when life keeps breaking your heart

when grief keeps knocking at your ribs

when pain keeps attending your soul

{ UNinvited }

r e m e m b e r

you are not failing

you are human

what if i don't want to be

the strong one anymore

even if just for tonight

what if i want to break into

a million tiny pieces

on the bedroom floor

to be found

carefully swept up

and held

until every piece of me

fuses back together again

let me fall apart

in case no one has told you

it's okay to feel your pain

without trying to find meaning in it

— on suffering

scars kiss my skin
telling a silent story
of survival

come,
won't you sit a while with me
tell me all the things
you should have said

if you care the way you say you do
sit with me a while
while i show you just
a little sliver of my pain

and if you can't
if you let your eyes fall instead of meeting mine
keep your words and tie them into knots
taste their hollow flavor on your tongue

if you can't sit a while with the broken
stay in your castle
behind its cold walls
and don't think of me at all

love can not exist amongst

the reeds of unforgiveness

it withers and fades

until all you hold is

a vague recollection of fondness

a ghost from a once happier past

—forgive and set love free

imperfections paint you real

scars colour you alive

they show you have lived

you have lived

you have lived

sometimes the weight
of this melancholy soul
feels too heavy for this world

let's create another

you see one tear

but i see

an entire ocean

and i will hold you

as you learn to swim

this sea of grief

gentlestrength

i sat across from my younger self the other day

she was more than a little surprised to see me

her eyes were so wide as she searched mine

i told her some of what would come

she didn't believe me, but she listened all the same

i held her hands in mine and told her how i loved her

how she was so much more valuable than she realized

she rolled her eyes and looked away, then came back to meet mine

had no one ever told her how she is enough

that her quiet, gentle way, and her different outlook

were lovable and perfectly okay

of course they had, but perhaps this would be the day she would believe

i felt a tear come to the corner of my eye as i thought of all she would endure

i spared that part, not wanting to break her heart

i finally settled on what to say

trust yourself and trust your heart

your softness is a gift, not the curse you believe it to be

even if you accomplished nothing more than you have today

you are worthy and exceptional in your own way

be kind to yourself

don't let your mistakes define you

make room for fun and for joy

even in the midst of pain

freedom will find you one day soon

be sure to take hold of it

rest in it

and while there will be days you will believe

you won't make it through

you are so much stronger than you know

live by grace

not by fear

on days my soul needs rest

to breathe is simply enough

—— on grace

i will remain soft
in a world marked by hardness

i long for nothing more than this

to remain a soft place

for the world to rest her head

c o m p a s s i o n rests its

head in my lap and reminds me

even the most unkind people

need kindness, too.

with each new morning

may hope rise with the sun

and never set on our hearts

—hope rising

hope lets the light in
small and wild, gently it blooms
guiding your heart home

less rushing, more *lingering*

less distraction, more *noticing*

less comparison, more *gratitude*

and so

i'm letting the distance

between where i am

and where i am going

be all the s p a c e

i need to

g r o W

it may be what broke you open

but it is also what made you

notice

m o r e

be present

m o r e

love

m o r e

My bones tell a
story of survival;
my heart sings a
song of hope.

for all the words you've never spoken
i feel them all the same

i will fall

but i will allow

every soft place

i land to

hold me

a little while

cominghome

i am lost and found in

the folds of this longing

seen and known in the

fibers of this belonging

you are not lost

you have been

searching for home

in someone else

and forgotten

it is in y o u

your outline

in the dark

—*my home*

what if your purpose is not some big thing outside yourself

what if it is a small, quiet one nestled between your ribs

given just enough space to flourish

with just enough spark to light a fire

and just enough joy to start a revolution

what if you have been given just enough breath

to breathe your purpose

and the truth is

i'm getting more

c o m f o r t a b l e

letting others down

when it means

i'm no longer

letting *myself*

d

o

w

n

when your heart

feels restless

remember

—you are home

Resistance meets me in my braver moments, reminding me of all my fears. Whispering *you don't belong here.* But my bones, they tell another story. A story of survival, a song of hope. One that seeks to echo once I'm no longer here. And that's enough to set me free. To be the woman I long to be.

i will not let past stamp

expectant pain on present

nor let indifference make me cold

i will not let yesterday's hurt cause me

to miss moments longing to be known

i will hold on to myself

i will

    {{hold}}

        on to

            myself

i will not dissolve into lost time

and unmade memories

i will *lean in* to moments

    until a moment i become

let my mind be

a safe haven and

not a battleground

i want to linger longer
in the spaces that
breathe deep joy
into my bones

i wonder if

success is simply

this:

housing a heart that remains open

when life gives it every reason

to close

cynicism   is

contagious, but

so is hope

i will hold you until

life feels lighter

and the world a little kinder

to watch you learn
and to watch you grow
is the greatest gift
i will ever know

About the Author

Melissa Anderson is a Canadian-based writer living in Alberta with her husband and two daughters. She began writing as a young girl and found her way back to it later in life as a way of healing after receiving a life-altering cancer diagnosis as a teenager. The years following were filled with treatments and many surgeries, and, ultimately, Melissa survived against all odds after being given an end-stage diagnosis. But the promise of a future and a family stayed with her and a miracle occurred that her doctor had never seen before: Melissa made a full recovery and a few years later went on to start a family with her husband after being told she may never have children.

Melissa began to write in a different way than she ever had before. This time, to heal. She began to share her work on Instagram and in literary journals as a way to connect with others and fell in love with the creative process. She has a deep love of nature and has no greater gratitude and joy than when she is hiking, travelling, or spending time outdoors with her family and her dog, and nature is a common theme throughout her writing.

In June 2023, Melissa received another shocking blow when she was diagnosed with ovarian cancer. Often little-known, childhood cancers and their treatments place individuals at significantly higher risk of secondary cancers later in life. Melissa learned she had been unknowingly living with cancer for many years, despite being otherwise healthy and active as a runner. Writing became a lifeline. A daily practice of gratitude and grounding. A safe place to put down every fear, worry, experience, and joy. It continues to help her as she is on this journey of living with cancer and in constant treatment. Her experiences have given her a unique perspective on life and an ability to find beauty in everyday moments, even the mundane, and she writes daily of the beauty she sees all around her. She hopes for all of us to be come noticers of unnoticed things.

As a two-time cancer survivor, she is no stranger to tragedy and suffering; however, daily she chooses to live fully and joyfully even in the cracks of it all. Her biggest message is that we are not defined by what happens to us, but rather by our responses to what happens. That we can choose how we show up in even the most difficult situations. Faith and gratitude are the cornerstones of her life, and her one hope is that would come through in her words.